An Orchid's Guide to Life

poems by

Kathryn Jones

Finishing Line Press
Georgetown, Kentucky

An Orchid's Guide to Life

ACKNOWLEDGMENTS

Many thanks to the editors of the following journals and anthologies for publishing four of the poems ("Castaway at Midnight," "Murmuration," "Spiral World," and "Orchids in April") included in this book:

TejasCovido.com
TexasPoetryAssignment.org
Lone Star Poetry (Kallisto Gaia Press, 2022)
Last Stanza Poetry Journal, Issue 14 (Last Stanza Poetry Association, 2023)

Publisher: Leah Huete de Maines
Editor: Christen Kincaid
Cover Art: David Valdez
Author Photo: Dan Malone
Cover Design: Elizabeth Maines McCleavy

Order online: www.finishinglinepress.com
also available on amazon.com

Author inquiries and mail orders:
Finishing Line Press
PO Box 1626
Georgetown, Kentucky 40324
USA

Contents

In memory of my father, Samuel Andrew Jones,
who taught me to see beauty in unlikely places

Family Pictures

My mother holds me in her arms;
she looks so thin in a dark dress
a month after childbirth.
My father smiles down at me,
hand on her shoulder in a
black-and-white photo with
a vintage scalloped border
torn across the left corner.

In another photo I smile,
blond hair not yet turned brown,
pink dress with puffed sleeves,
holding onto a rocking horse,
juniper trees framing me,
wildflower in my tiny hand,
my three-year-old self staring at it,
transfixed, unaware of the camera.

I have no memory of that spring day,
no idea what happened to the rocking horse,
what kind of wildflower it was.
I don't recognize that girl at all,
but in her was a seed planted
by that beauty, by the love
of people who are gone now—
self, soul, a poem I hold inside.

As I sit on their bed going through
the polished mahogany box of family pictures,
I turn over each one, read the names
of friends and relatives long vanished—
places, dates, handwritten comments.
Now the box is mine; my mother wanted me to have it
not only for the pictures, but mainly
so I can be the keeper of memory.

The Orchid Keeper

Ranunculus arrived first in the garden.
My father planted the bulbs in rich soil,
in a location with full sun. They bloomed
the very next spring. I studied the rose-pink ones,
layers of ruffled petals arranged in a spiral—
such perfection in an imperfect world.

Then he planted roses in raised beds:
austere scarlet Mister Lincoln;
romantic red climbers named Don Juan;
pale lavender Sterling Silver, gaudy coral Tropicana,
elegant white Tranquility. My world revolved
around flowers, color, soft petals, fragrance.

One day a friend gave my father a potted orchid—
a Phalaenopsis, also known as a moth orchid.
Unlike Ranunculus or roses, the orchid opened itself up
to passion, luring pollinators inside its ruffled pink lips.
He doted on the plant, watering it every other day.
The orchid died.

My father learned from books that wild orchids
attach themselves to trees and rocks, or grow
on forest floors, even in desert canyons.
They do not like to have wet roots.
That was the epiphany: give orchids space, air,
water only when dry—just enough but not too much.

After that first orchid, he was smitten, hooked, obsessed.
He built a greenhouse, came to know the orchids as individuals,
their names, desires, quirks. In turn, they gave him what he
needed—a place of stillness, a sanctuary. He was not their owner,
creator, only their keeper, he told me. He tended the orchids but,
even more, the orchids tended him.

Still Life with Loquats

How often during the summer I escaped
from our noisy house of chattering children
and quarreling parents to the backyard
where two loquat trees grew side by side,
glossy veined leaves weaving a tarpaulin
so thick that grass could not grow underneath
but I could, spending hours daydreaming,
reading, exulting in the luxury
of stillness.

Under the loquat trees I listened
to the woodpeckers rat-a-tat-tatting,
to sprinklers hissing in the neighbor's yard,
to the low murmur of bees,
to mockingbirds squawking in the trees,
mobbing the clusters of tart-sweet loquats
also called Japanese plums, tough to peel
but such an exotic tropical flavor
like a drop of sunshine on my tongue.
I learned loquats were native to China,
then raised in Japan for a thousand years.
They transported me to faraway places
beyond the redwood fence that formed
the border of my sheltered life.

Decades later when I visited Japan,
I saw a painting in a Tokyo gallery—
a tiny mountain bird perched
on a loquat branch with a cluster of fruit.
I felt such longing for the cool shade
under the loquats on the other side of the world,
that shelter of place, those tangy-sweet
drops of sunshine on my tongue,
but mostly I longed for that stillness.

Midnight in the Greenhouse of Desire

That summer night we wanted to admire
orchids in the moonlight.
Inside the greenhouse the moist air
smelled fecund, felt heavy with longing.
A kiss led to another and then more.

Their bright faces watched us so intently,
exposing their voluptuous petals,
their quivering lips and sticky tongues
designed for pollination,
desiring of at least a threesome.

They open themselves to discovery
by tiny feet and hairy bodies
probing, groping, searching
their secret places, fulfilling their
one true purpose—to be touched.

I closed my eyes, felt breath and skin
against me as the orchids nodded their blessing,
my back pressed against the wooden table
where I'd gently pushed the pots aside
and felt their earthy dampness.

I opened my eyes, saw my lover's face above mine,
not adoring but indifferent, then felt a rush
of regret. I left the orchids in the moonlight
luring their suitors—a bee, a moth, an ant—
with deliberate intent and no regrets, ever.

How I envy them, blooming day and night,
their beauty fresh and glistening,
worshipped in their house of water and light,
their desire satisfied while tonight
I will be alone in my house, petals dry, untouched.

The Nautilus Heart

Pearly, secret chambers
pump seawater in and out,
letting you swim without tail or fins,
propelling you through life
like a heart beating in a hard shell,
unbreakable.

Ancient Greeks saw perfection
in your chambers: logarithmic spiral,
Dürer's "eternal line," like a hurricane,
a galaxy, Half Moon Bay,
the way a hawk circles prey
or a spider spins a web.
.

Divine design threatened,
ripped out of your shell for
nacre, hard and iridescent like a pearl,
perfect for cheap tourist trinkets,
or your whole shell put on display
like a piece of sculpture.

A living fossil, you survived extinctions,
but now you face a formidable predator,
not of the sea but of the land
with a multi-chambered heart
beating in a hard shell,
broken.

Memory Is Elusive

In my parents' bedroom, I open the cedar chest,
the lid heavier than I remember.
I used to love the smell and hear her exclaim
as she pulled out some object of remembrance—
my faded pink baby dress and matching bonnet,
old postcards from a train trip to California,
a black velvet evening jacket with swirls of gold sequins,
yellowed newspaper clippings with names circled,
a silver charm bracelet with a tiny Eiffel Tower
even though she never got to see France.

Buried beneath the clippings,
her diary in a brown leather cover,
worn along the edges, brass lock missing a key,
lined pages edged in red,
January and February falling out of the binding.
Printed at the top of the first page, an inscription:
"Memory is elusive. Capture it."
She filled the pages with her meticulous cursive,
writing some entries in pencil, some in blue ink,
some in green, documenting her days and nights.

In the diary she was not my mother,
just a seventeen-year-old girl going to school,
to the movies or dancing with dates,
roller skating with friends,
wondering why a certain boy didn't call her,
reports of hands held, a few kisses exchanged—
innocence, joy, and disappointments in the pages.
She spent one New Year's Eve home alone.
"It was a terrible night," she wrote.
I felt her pain from across the decades.

I saw my mother not as a woman who died
cursing at invisible demons, but as a gentle soul
twirling on a dance floor, dreaming of the future
before marriage, a divorce, another marriage,
three children, illnesses, isolation, bitterness,
and a long slide into mental illness.
I kept the charm bracelet and the evening jacket
but my most valuable heirloom is the diary
so I can read about the girl I never knew
and wish I did.

The Peach Tree

He sits in the chair,
then stands, draws the curtains shut.
The yard once green, now brown,
feels like his heart.

Tissue in one hand, remote in the other,
he gazes at images flashing across the screen
but does not see them.
Her chair is empty.

His daughters clean the house,
cook his meals, wash, mow,
pull weeds around the gaping hole
that used to be a lily pond.

He dug the hole by hand,
lined it with brick, filled it with water.
Lilies floated on the surface;
goldfish glinted in the shadows.

He holds a photo frayed around the edges:
they stood by the pond, his hand on her shoulder,
smiling in the sun as plumeria bloomed
behind them, raining pink petals.

He brought her an orchid from the greenhouse
every week, snipping a blooming spike
or pinching off a single blossom.
It always lasted for weeks.

She fell and quit going outside.
He had to help her walk, dress her, feed her.
Water lilies withered, goldfish rotted
in the mud. He gave away the orchids.

The daughters pry up the pond's bricks,
pull up the plastic liner caked with mud,
trash, and muck. They want to fill the hole.
"Let's plant a tree," they suggest.

He shakes his head "no." They grab a shovel,
ladle soil into the hole. "What kind?" they ask.
Wind kicks up a memory.
He pauses. "Peach," he says.

Later he draws open the curtains.
The sapling stands in a mound of mulch.
He sits in her chair, waits for spring,
for pink blossoms, and for fruit.

Orchid's Guide to Life

Do not put me in the ground
like a common dirt plant—

my roots will suffocate or drown;
they must dangle and breathe.

Look up at the rain forest canopy,
where tree branches tremble in the wind,

or at a desert canyon wall
where a spring seeps from cracks—

there my roots cling to limbs, rocks, crevices,
embracing the home offered to me.

I survive, I thrive not by fearing hardship or change,
but by knowing how to live in hostile places,

taking sustenance from air, water, sun, tree bark,
transforming, unfurling, becoming,

fulfilling my destiny—to send up a flower spike,
reach for the light, and bloom.

Vuelve a La Vida (Come Back to Life)

Passed away,
went home to be with Jesus,
departed this Earth,
crossed the River Jordan,
left this mortal realm,
kicked the bucket,
bit the dust,
gave up the ghost,
crossed the Great Divide,
met his Maker,
went to a better place,
lost his battle with cancer.

My father did all of those things;
can it be only five years ago
since he died—yes, he died,
so let's drop the cloaked language.
Why obscure, why deny,
why dance around the truth?
He died and it was not peaceful,
it was not meant to be,
it was not for the best.

Let me tell you what it was like, his dying—
he lost his appetite, then his strength;
he lost his ability to walk,
to dress himself;
he lost control of his bowels,
asked me, his eldest daughter,
to clean the shit off his penis
when I took off the diaper
so at least he would not lose that dignity.
Then he lost his desire to have any dignity.
I cleaned him anyway.

Finally, he lost the power to talk,
lying in the hospital bed set up
in the paneled den of my parents' home
where they used to watch TV reruns every night.
He slipped into a morphine trance,
staring at the ceiling, eyes a dim gray,
faded from their original brown like mine.
What are you looking at, my father?
Do you see our mother?
Do you see Jesus? A light? A ladder?
A spider crawling on the ceiling fan?
He did not answer.
He lost his color.
His face turned white.
His feet turned blue.
His eyes closed forever.

After the funeral, I went back to my life
although I did not return to it.
I got up, worked, came home, drank a glass of wine—
sometimes two. Three. Four.
Watched some mindless TV, went to bed,
did it all over again the next day, and the next.
I prayed, but my words echoed in a cavity.
I drifted, anchorless. There are sayings for that, too:
in a funk,
hit with the gloomies,
feeling blue,
mired in melancholy,
having a downer of a day,
or the less polite version—screwed up.

One day I heard a voice whisper to me:
"Vuelve a la vida."
Come back to life.
Shake it off.
Get up and go.
Seize the day.
Return to joy. To beauty. To peace.
Find your joie de vivre.
Bloom again.
I looked down at my hands, constructed
so much like my father's. I grasped one
with the other in an embrace.
They whispered to each other,
I will try. I will try.

The Closing

I walked through my childhood home
for the last time with a stranger who
bought it at a cheap price to sell
to other people I will never know.
It felt like a tomb of a house,
dead without any people living
in the rooms. The new owner said it needed
a new roof, plumbing, electrical work,
old carpet ripped up, tile replaced.
Mainly it needed more joy, fewer tears.

I took the brass key off the metal ring,
the key that unlocked the door
when I tiptoed in after midnight
when I was supposed to be in by eleven;
the key I duplicated so I could let myself in
when my dying father was too ill to open the door,
the key that meant I had two homes even
after I married, that I was still someone's child.

Now an orphan handed the key to the stranger.
He put it in a lock box, hung it on the doorknob
so other strangers could cross the threshold.
I stood there on the porch steps, thought I saw a face
but there was no one at the window.
Only the elm tree in the front yard
waved its branches at me.

There was no one to tell goodbye.
I got in my car, put it in reverse, paused,
took a breath. Then I raised the invisible anchor,
backed out of the driveway into what used to be
my street, and watched my childhood
fade away in the rear-view mirror.

Aubade at the Bronze Wall of Names

In this cemetery
each stone I step across
on the way to your tomb

looks colder
than the morning fog
hanging above the bay.

I bought a single red rose
at the florist shop
so I could mark the place

where you sleep hidden
but you're up so high,
just a name on a bronze plaque.

The last time I saw you,
your hands were folded,
my Father's Day card next to you

before the crane took you
up, up, up, thrust you into
darkness, sealed for eternity.

I don't know whether to
shout a greeting or throw a stone.
Would you even hear the ping?

I hear your voice tending
the orchids you left blooming
in the greenhouse:

Don't water them too much,
they're not dirt plants
they live in bark or cling to a tree,

epiphytes, receiving
all they need from air
and water and rain.

I place the rose on the ground,
look up as the sun pushes through,
highlighting your name,

then I feel your roots dangling
like an epiphyte attached to the wall,
reaching for morning.

The Edge of Ambedo

All day worldly terrors gnaw at me;
the blinking screen screams war, pandemic,
murder, madness. Lost souls swirl
in a murmuration of chaos.

I flee outside into the wild peace.
A Monarch flutters from flower to flower,
probing purple mistflower for nectar.
Fly, alight, sip; fly, alight, sip.

Delicate wings bear me to the edge of ambedo.
I step off and float like a butterfly over the abyss.
The Monarch shows me how to find sustenance.
Fly, alight, suck life's sweetness before it vanishes.

Insomnia

Be still, my unquiet mind;
do not go down that dark hallway,
doors on each side half open,
beckoning me to enter
rooms with faces floating in the wallpaper,
echoes and creaks and a stifled scream—
I have been there too many times.

I close my eyes, pray for sleep.
Outside the moon slides below the clouds,
throws a dagger of light across my face.
My eyes flutter open; I look out the window.
A shadow creature rustles in the garden;
irises sway like violet ghosts.
I toss back the covers.

It's coming.

I get up, go to the kitchen, pour a glass of water.
An invisible icy hand rests on my shoulder;
I shudder and wrap myself in a robe.
The clock ticks, the pendulum swings,
the kitchen faucet drips and so does my mind,
counting off the things I must do tomorrow
but tomorrow is already today.

I surrender and retreat to bed.
The moon sets, the rays no longer pierce my pillow.
The garden is still, the wind chimes tinkle.
The doors close, the faces fade into the wallpaper.
I fall into a deep sleep and dream...
artists paint naked people in a strange room;
spies chase me with guns; I'm sick in a hospital
with a tube down my throat. I run to the edge
of an abyss and start falling, falling, falling....

I jolt awake, soaked with sweat,
relieved to see sunlight and a brief reprieve.
Then the afternoon shadows lengthen,
the day dwindles again,
the carousel begins spinning in my head,
horses frozen in gallop, nostrils flared,
chasing each other around in circles.
I hold on, eyes shut, but I do not sleep.

Bird's Eye View

I hear faint cries high in the sky
on the first chilly day of fall,
long to fly away and join them,
to hitchhike on beating wings,
align with sandhill cranes in flight,
sun and wind on my back,
head by instinct to a place I know—
but when I get there, it's changed
and I change it again with my presence,
then return in early spring to find
the refuge I sought was here,
in this place, all along.

Murmuration

We swarm
    a flock of individuals
        a collective with no leader
            aligning with no rhyme
                revolving with no reason
            pulsating like a heartbeat
    whirling like a sprite in flight

We do not touch
    or collide but ripple like a wave
        float like a vessel on a current
            sail like a kite on a river of wind

They ask
    whether it's intelligence or instinct
        they study how we should behave
            employ their algorithms
                their models and theories but
        they do not begin to explain us

We express
    our nature, our winged joy together
        yet apart, defying logic, predictability
    geese fly in V-formation

We fly
        in swirls that start   and stop   and start again
            drawing arabesques in the sky
                ebbing, flowing
                    in the ocean of air
            then
We disappear
    like a black star
        no sound but the beating of
            a thousand wings
        mingling into
  a murmur

To My Father's Orchids

Tell me,
please tell me what he did
to make you bloom,
to convince you to send up a tender stem,
to open your buds and reveal such splendor,
to make your roots crawl out of their pots,
to dangle like fingers reaching for the light.
Whisper the secrets you told him about beauty
so he never lost faith you would bloom again.
Turn your faces to me—some flat, some with a ruffled lip,
some with fringed petals, some striped, some spotted—
tell me how you all came to thrive in this place
and bloom—bloom!—for him but not for me.
You do not have any choice now, do you understand?
He is gone and not coming back, your caretaker, your god.
He left all of you to me, despite—perhaps because of—
my shortcomings, so I would have something to tend.
Now your fleshy green leaves sag—are you grieving as I am?
Take heart that he loved you like children,
showered on you his time, energy, devotion.
Now I really need to know: What makes you bloom?
Can you please, please, please
tell me?

Hanging Gardens

If grief were a landscape
it would look like
a desert canyon where
I saw spring water dripping
down a stone wall,
trailing dark streaks
like tracks of dirty tears.
How could so little water
make much difference
in such an arid place,
I wondered, but then I looked up
and saw hanging gardens—
moss and ferns sprouting
from rock crevices, lush spots
of green against brown,
dangling hope that love could
take root again in my arid heart.

Wild Solace

This world of doors, of rooms with no views,
of lights in the ceiling instead of sun and sky
leaves me choking on dust, gasping for air.

When darkness falls, I fling off my clothes,
becoming naked like an animal,
unlocking the door, plunging into blue moonlight.

Coyotes howl, owls hoot, night creatures
join the chirping, screeching chorus,
beckoning me to join them in the wild solace.

Soft grass caresses bare feet, lushness envelops me;
I breathe in the pure night smells of earth cooling,
of distant rain carried on the wind.

I feel unseen hearts beating, eyes staring in the dark.
Let me lie here, let me die here in the wild tangle
instead of a room with no windows, gasping for air.

Spiral World

With the tip of my pen
I draw a point on a blank page,
then a circle, unclosed.
A silent force takes my hand,
and the pen goes around and around
until I'm inside a fiddlehead fern unfurling,
a snail winding into a fragile shell,
water spinning in a whirlpool,
a dust devil skipping across the desert,
a hurricane pirouetting into the Gulf.

At Mesa Verde ancestral Puebloans
painted Tularosa swirls in black and white
on the bellies of clay pots.
Ancient ones in the desert Southwest
carved spirals into stone.
In Texas Tonkawa women painted
concentric circles on their bare breasts.
Sacred symbol, secret key
unlocking universal truths,
corkscrewing in and out of time,
orbiting with planets around stars,
swirling with galaxies into the celestial soup,
uncovering the passage from inner to outer,
human to divine.

There's no beginning, no end,
to this spiral world, only
an eternal coiling and uncoiling,
an infinite spool winding and unwinding.
Death is but an entry point into the force
that spins forever and that exists
for a few moments on a blank page
that I hold in my hand.

Orchids in April

It sits on the windowsill, soaking up light.
Green leaves as thick as leather,
roots creeping out of the pot
like thin, bony fingers
searching for something to grasp.

Every spring, flower spikes shoot up,
buds swell, and the orbs burst open,
unfurling flat white petals like moth wings
and a crimson lip that juts out, begging
an insect to taste the sweetness inside.

Orchid blooms last for weeks without
much tending and so must I,
soaking up light by the window.
My bony fingers creep out of my vessel,
searching for something to grasp.

I reach out and touch the rubescent lip—
such tenderness, such fearlessness
to bloom in this world right now.
My raw heart opens and beauty holds out
her hand. With gratitude, I grasp it.

Kathryn Jones is a longtime journalist and essayist whose writing has appeared in *The New York Times, Texas Monthly,* and in books about music, film, and literature, most recently *Pastures of the Empty Page: Fellow Writers on the Life and Legacy of Larry McMurtry* (University of Texas Press, 2023). Her poetry has been published in numerous literary journals and anthologies, including *Odes and Elegies: Eco-Poetry from the Texas Gulf Coast* (Lamar University Literary Press, 2020), *Unknotting the Line: The Poetry in Prose* (Dos Gatos Press, 2023), *and Lone Star Poetry* (Kallisto Gaia Press, 2023). Jones was inducted into the Texas Institute of Letters and lives on a ranch near Glen Rose, Texas.

www.ingramcontent.com/pod-product-compliance
Lightning Source LLC
Chambersburg PA
CBHW022058080426
42734CB00009B/1403